GUIDE TO MILITARY UNIFORMS

Andrew Kershaw

Illustrated by Pete Robinson

Ray Rourke Publishing Company, Inc.
Windermere, Florida 32786

Published by Ray Rourke Publishing Company, Inc.,
Windermere, Florida 32786.

Library of Congress Cataloging in Publication Data

Kershaw, Andrew.
  Guide to military uniforms.

  (Explorer guides)
  Includes index.
  SUMMARY: An illustrated guide to uniforms
from antiquity to the present day.
  1. Uniforms, Military—Juvenile literature.
[1. Uniforms, Military]   I. Robinson, Pete.
II. Title.   III. Series.
UC480.K4   1981   355.1'4   81-890
ISBN 0-86592-023-0   AACR2

From left to right: Officer of
the Chevaux-Légers de Berg
Regiment of Saxony (1808).
Frankish warrior (6th
century). Dismounted
Norman knight (1066).
British Yeoman Warder of
the Tower of London (1975).
US Confederate Navy
captain (1862). French
Foreign Legion corporal
(1942). Female Cambodian
guerilla (1980).

Contents

The First Uniforms	4
The Middle Ages	6
Uniforms for Show	8
Napoleonic Wars	10
The New Warfare	12
Uniforms at Sea	14
World War I	16
World War II	18
Today's Uniforms	20
Ceremonial	22
Glossary	23
Index	24

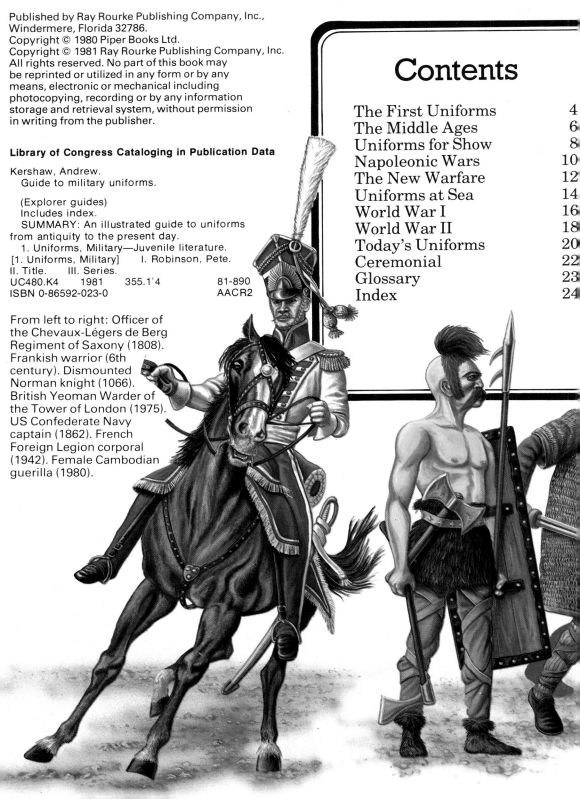

About This Book

In the early days of warfare there were no uniforms. Soldiers just wore the most practical clothes they had, with whatever armor they could collect. In large battles, however, uniforms helped each side to tell friend from foe. They also gave the soldiers a sense of comradeship and loyalty.

There have been many types of uniforms. Styles have ranged from the very elaborate uniforms of the 18th century, to the practical, hardwearing styles of today. But the uniforms of every age can tell a story of the times in which they were worn.

The First Uniforms

When soldiers fought with shields and spears, they wore light armor. This protected them but still allowed them to move easily in hand-to-hand battles. The shapes of their helmet and armor and the design on their shields distinguished one side from the other.

The soldiers shown here all fought in highly organised armies.

Persian infantry (left) engage in battle with Greek infantry (called hoplites) in the 4th century BC. Helmets and tunics formed the main part of both sides' uniforms.

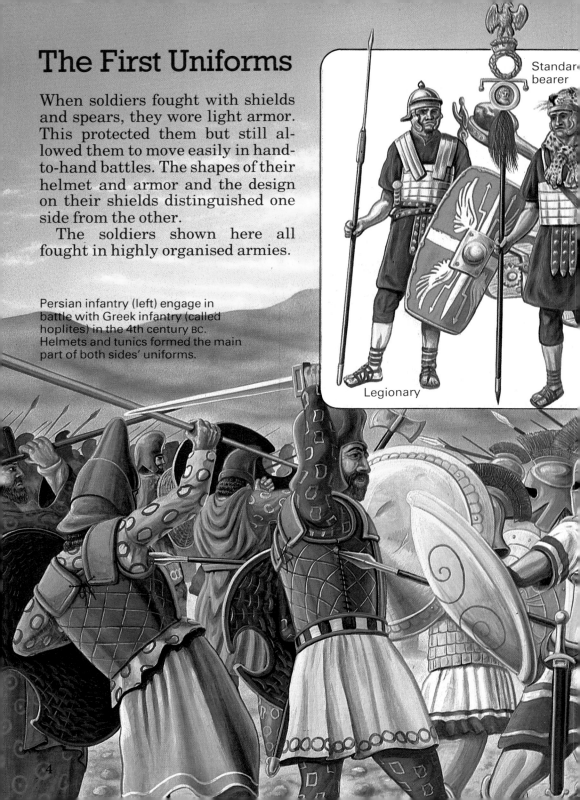

Standard bearer

Legionary

4

ROMANS

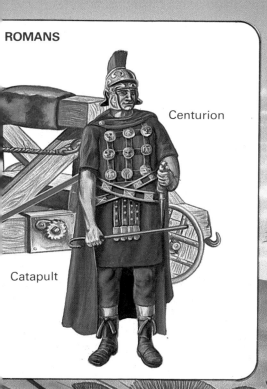

Centurion

Catapult

FAR EAST

Chinese cavalryman

Japanese Samurai

EGYPTIANS

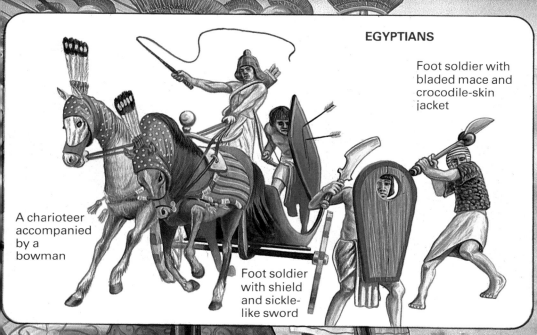

Foot soldier with bladed mace and crocodile-skin jacket

A charioteer accompanied by a bowman

Foot soldier with shield and sickle-like sword

The Middle Ages

Under the feudal system, knights who were given land had to raise and equip an army when needed. The knights fought on horseback and wore heavy armor. The infantry wore helmets and tunics.

The scene shown here is from the Hundred Years War (1337–1453). English longbowmen and pikemen fought against mounted French knights and archers with crossbows. The longbow proved to be the best weapon until firearms were introduced. In later battles armor became less important.

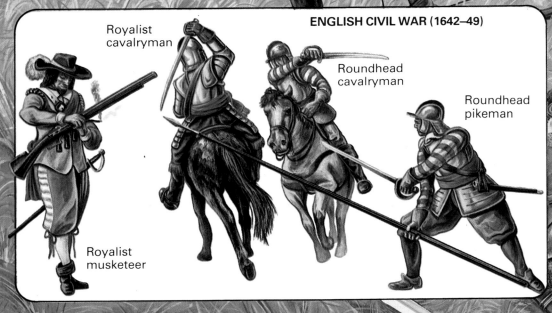

ENGLISH CIVIL WAR (1642–49)

Royalist cavalryman

Roundhead cavalryman

Roundhead pikeman

Royalist musketeer

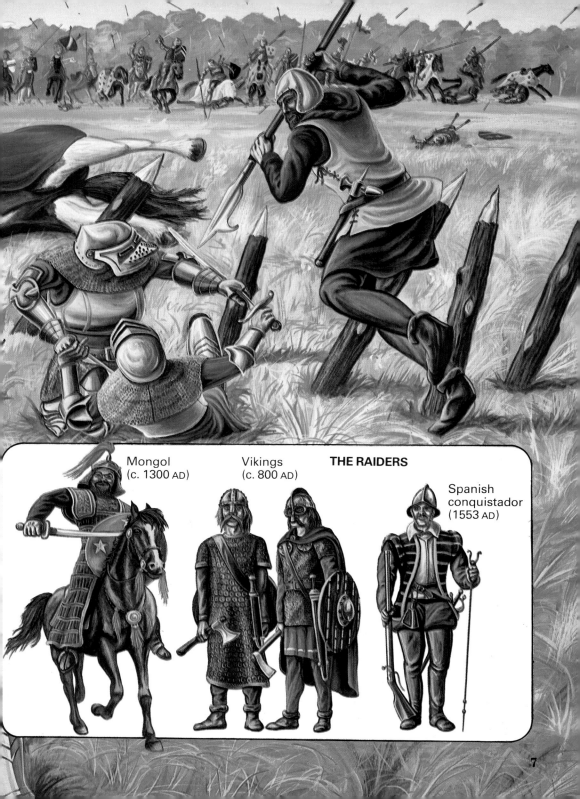

THE RAIDERS

Mongol
(c. 1300 AD)

Vikings
(c. 800 AD)

Spanish
conquistador
(1553 AD)

Uniforms for Show

In the 18th century, the army was a fashionable career for rich aristocrats. Many regiments were founded by lords who equipped their soldiers in elaborate and distinctive uniforms.

Soldiers felt great pride and loyalty towards their own regiment. Small armies of professional soldiers were common.

Soldiers like these below helped to crush the Scots who rebelled against British rule in 1715 and 1745. They are a Black Watch corporal and a German in British service – a Hessen-Kassel grenadier.

The War of Austrian Succession (1740-48) involved most of the states of Europe. Although each state tended to follow one particular style of uniform for each branch of its army, each regiment's dress still varied considerably.

Austrian captain of cuirassiers

Prussian grenadie and

FRENCH REVOLUTION (1789–95)

National Guard grenadier

Royalist Swiss Guard

WAR OF AUSTRIAN SUCCESSION

...nbadier

French dragoon

British infantry private

Austrian infantry private

Dutch Pioneer guardsman

AMERICAN WAR OF INDEPENDENCE (1775–83)

British 14th Foot private

American 1st Georgia Regiment private

American Washington Guards

Austrian Slavonian Frontier Regiment private

Austro-Hungarian musketeer

Baden grenadier

SEVEN YEARS WAR

The Seven Years War (1756-63) was a struggle between various German-speaking European states and their allies.

Prussian "Death's Head" hussar

French hussar

Schaumburg-Lippe carabinier

Napoleonic Wars

Between 1804 and 1815, France, under Napoleon's brilliant leadership, took on nearly the whole of Europe . . . and very nearly won. The fighting involved millions of soldiers. As a result, uniforms had to be made in great numbers.

Napoleon's army included more than a million conscripted men. Conscription was used in much of Europe, and the tactics used in battle had to be changed to suit large armies of untrained men.

Soldiers in panel below, from left to right: British 3rd Dragoons trooper, Prussian grenadier, Brunswick Black Corps private, French Imperial Guard 2nd Conscrit-Chasseurs sapper, French Imperial Guard foot artilleryman, French captain, Russian infantry musketeer, French 3rd Hussars, French Mameluke private (North African), French Light Infantry cantiniere, French Imperial Guard dragoon.

French Westphalian cuirassier

Fren Poli lanc

British 93rd Highlanders private

British
hussar

French
Imperial
Guard
fusilier

French Imperial
Guard (bearer)

French Imperial
Guard grenadier

British
King's
German
Legion
corporal

The New Warfare

Warfare changed dramatically during the 19th century. With the introduction of rifled barrels and breech-loading cartridges, firearms became deadly accurate.

Towards the end of the century, uniforms became less elaborate and more practical. Drab colors such as khaki and field gray replaced the showy scarlets of before.

This scene from the American Civil War (1861-65) shows a Federal field artillery conscript slumped against his gun, a Federal infantry conscript dead on the ground, with a Confederate infantry conscript sitting over him. Approaching from the right is a Confederate cavalry corporal of "Hampton's Legion", followed by a Confederate Zouave of the famous French-speaking "Louisiana Tigers".

FRANCO PRUSSIAN WAR (1870-71)

French cuirassier trooper

Prussian Garde-Regiment private

THE BALKAN WARS (1912-13)

Turkish private

Bosnian mountain soldier

CRIMEAN WAR (1854-56)

Russian infantry private

British 89th Foot

French grenadier corporal

British 17th Lancers

Russian Caucasian Rifles lance corporal

RUSSO-JAPANESE WAR (1904-05)

Russian infantry private

Japanese infantry guards private

MEXICAN WAR (1846-48)

US infantry conscript

Mexican 1st Regular Infantry private

Uniforms at Sea

Like army uniforms, those of the world's navies have become less elaborate over the years. For the officers, frock coats, knee-breeches, and tricorne hats have been replaced by simple jackets, trousers and peaked caps. Most other ranks wear smocks with large square collars.

The main picture shows a scene on board a British ship during the Battle of Trafalgar in 1805. Nelson was killed at this battle. In his showy uniform he was an easy target for the enemy.

US Marine Corps marine (1780)

British Royal Navy commander (1756)

French Navy commander (1763)

British officer of Marin

Royal Navy lieutenant

Royal Navy post-captain

French Naval Batt. I/corp. (1870)

Russian Navy commander (1905)

British Navy petty officer (1915)

Japanese Navy rating (1905)

Japanese Imperial Navy marine (1939)

Italian ''sea-pig'' human torpedo and frogmen crew

British Royal Navy rating (1970)

Kenyan Navy recruit (1963)

US Navy rating (1950)

German U-boat rating (1943)

World War I

Most of the fighting in World War I took place from trenches, often less than 300 feet apart. Many countries were involved. For the Mustard gas and tanks were used for the first time. Soldiers had to carry gas masks at all times. Tanks and armored vehicles were operated by cavalry regiments who used horses only for reconnaissance.

US infantry conscript (1917)

German infantry private (1917)

German artillery officer (1916)

British Highlander private (1916)

first time each service had one basic uniform, and officers' uniforms looked like those of ordinary soldiers. Any officer who stood out would have made an easy target for an enemy sharpshooter. Only cap badges and flashes were used to distinguish a soldier's rank and regiment.

Australian private (1915)

Prussian infantry private (1914)

Turkish officer (1916)

Russian infantry private (1914)

British infantry lance-corporal (1915)

French infantry private (1916)

World War II

Uniforms changed little between the two World Wars, but weapons and tactics changed considerably. Soldiers were equipped with bazookas, sub-machine guns and automatic rifles. Army, naval and air force units fought in combined operations. Soldiers and artillery on the ground were supported by fighter and bomber air strikes.

German Afrika Korps private

British 8th Army "Desert Rat" private

Russian female pilot

British infantry private

German Panzer (tank) officer

US infantry private

British
Chindit
(Burma)

Japanese
infantry
private

Gurkha
infantryman
from
Nepal

Japanese
"kamikaze"
pilot

German
Wehrmacht
officer

German
infantry
private

German
paratrooper
corporal

19

Today's Uniforms

World War II ended when two atom bombs were dropped on Japan. The threat of nuclear war has dominated the major powers ever since. Soldiers have become highly trained technicians. They have also continued to fight with conventional (non-nuclear) weapons. Guerilla warfare is common. Small groups fight independently, attacking civil and military targets. Regular army units rely on fast-moving armored vehicles and helicopters to fight them. Uniforms are lightweight and practical.

The picture on the right shows Russian infantrymen wearing summer battle uniforms and camouflaged overalls. Nowadays, most armies can be moved in fast, armored vehicles such as those shown here.

The picture below shows a British infantry sergeant operating controls to launch a Swingfire antitank missile.

Below: An RAF Phantom fighter-bomber pilot. His helmet contains radio systems. His suit is pressurised to help his body withstand the force of gravity as it increases during supersonic flight. His suit is also air-conditioned.

US Army "Green Berets" in Vietnam. This élite unit operated behind the enemy lines and themselves used guerilla tactics.

British troops in riot gear. They wear bulletproof vests and carry tough plastic riot shields.

This French Air Cavalry paratrooper is wearing a light camouflaged uniform which helps him to move around easily.

Ceremonial

Today's uniforms are strictly practical, but the old colorful uniforms have not been forgotten. They are still used by regiments on ceremonial occasions, and for performing special duties, such as guarding royal palaces and historic buildings.

All the uniforms shown on this page were once used as battle uniforms. These soldiers, however, wear modern army uniform when their ceremonial duties are over.

Swiss Guard of the Vatican State

Greek Royal Guard

British Army Scots Guard

British Army Life Guard

US Army West Point cadet in dress uniform

Palace Guard at the court of the King of Thailand

Glossary

Centurion An officer in the Roman army. He was in charge of a Century, a unit of between 60 and 80 men.

Cuirassier A mounted soldier who wore a cuirass or breastplate, and belonged to a division of heavy cavalry.

Dragoon A mounted infantry soldier who used his horse to get rapidly from place to place in battle.

Fusilier A soldier of the British army, formerly armed with a fusil—a light musket or firelock.

Grenadier Originally an infantry soldier who threw grenades. Now the word is used only in the name of the Grenadier Guards, the oldest foot regiment in the British Household Brigade.

Gurkha A soldier from Nepal in the British or Indian army.

Hussar A member of any European unit, originally modeled on the Hungarian Light Cavalry of the 15th century.

Kamikaze Japanese pilot of World War II who would deliberately crash his aircraft into the target, killing himself in the process.

Khaki Dull brownish yellow cloth used since 1899 for field uniforms.

Lancer A cavalryman armed with a lance. Lancer regiments were used by the British Army after 1816. Lancer regiments today are highly mechanised.

Musketeer A soldier armed with a musket. The musket was originally a match-lock gun, but the word is now used for any kind of old shoulder gun that is not a rifle.

Samurai The warrior aristocracy of Japan from the 12th to the 19th century. They followed a strict code of behavior called *bushido* (the way of the warrior).

Standard A flag or emblem carried on a pole to show the rallying point in battle.

Index

American Civil War 12, 13
American War of Independence 9
Australian private 17
Austrian cuirassiers 8
Austrian Slavonian Frontier Regiment 9
Austro-Hungarian infantry 9

Baden grenadier 9
Balkan Wars 12
Bosnian mountain soldier 12
Bowmen 5, 6
British uniforms 3, 6, 8, 9, 10, 11, 13, 14, 15, 16, 17, 18, 19, 20, 21, 22

Cambodian guerilla 3
Cavalry 5, 6
Centurian 5, 23
Ceremonial uniforms 22
Charioteer 5
Chevaux-Légers de Berg Regiment 2
China 5
Crimean War 13

Dutch Pioneer guardsman 9

Egypt 5
English Civil War 6

Franco Prussian War 12
Franks 2
French Revolution 8
French uniforms 3, 8, 9, 10, 11, 12, 13, 14, 15, 17, 21

German uniforms 15, 16, 18, 19
Greece 3, 4, 22
Greek Royal Guard 22
Gurkha 19, 23

Hessen-Kassel grenadier 8
Hoplites 4
Hundred Years War 6
Hungarian infantry 9

Italian frogmen 15

Japan 5, 13, 15, 19
Japanese "kamikaze" pilot 19, 23

Kenyan Navy 15
Knights 6

Legionary 4
Longbowmen 6

Mexican 1st Regular Infantry 13
Mexican War 13
Middle Ages 6
Mongol 7

Napoleonic Wars 10—11
National Guard grenadier (French) 8
Navy 3, 14—15
Normans 2

Palace Guard (Thailand) 22
Persia 3, 4
Pikemen 6, 7
Prussia 8, 10, 12
Prussian "Death's Head" hussar 9
Prussian infantry 17

RAF Phantom bomber pilot 20
Riot control 21
Rome 3, 4
Roundheads 6
Royalists 6

Royalist Swiss Guard 8
Russian uniforms 11, 13, 15, 17, 18, 20, 21
Russo-Japanese War 13

Samurai 5, 23
Saxony 2
Schaumburg-Lippe carabinier 9
Seven Years War 9
Spanish conquistador 7
Standard-bearer 4
Swiss Guard of Vatican State 22

Turkey 12, 17

US uniforms 3, 9, 12, 13, 14, 15, 16, 18, 21, 22

Vikings 7

War of Austrian Succession 8—9
World War I 16—17
World War II 18—19

Yeoman Warder of the Tower of London 3